'This book is a tremendous insight into the mind of
someone with borderline personality disorder; it
delves into the dark (and light) truths of the disorder,
revealing symptoms that so many encounter but very
few discuss. Each chapter shares deeply personal poems
which offer a far more abstract reflection of the author's
inner thoughts. They are a bittersweet reminder that
many mental health issues can uncover a creative
channel that can assist ongoing recovery and well-being.

This book reminds the reader that the BPD journey
does not begin and end in a specific place, but is a
continued path, difficult to follow yet walked by many.'
— *Lucy Spraggan, singer-songwriter*

'Tracy is a talented writer and poet, and this heartfelt
book will be of use and interest to anyone who suffers
from, or knows someone who suffers from, personality
disorder. The book is honest, engaging and upbeat –
Tracy shows her journey and the steps on the way to
a much happier and fulfilled life. The lows are very
low, but her strength, talent and determination shine
through, and anyone else feeling low can only be
inspired by her story. Highly recommended.'
— *Dan Knowles, CEO, Oxfordshire Mind*

'It was such a pleasure to read this book. It is beautifully
written, both the prose and the poetry. This is a
first-person account, from someone diagnosed with
personality disorder, which offers understanding and
hope and which will speak to many people.'
— *Dr Heather Castillo, independent consultant and author of*
Personality Disorder Temperament or Trauma? *and*
The Reality of Recovery in Personality Disorder

'This thoughtful and enormously readable book presents a valuable insight for clinical practitioners and for anyone impacted directly or indirectly by borderline personality disorder. The author offers a real opportunity to gain an understanding of both the emotional and clinical elements of borderline personality disorder. Her very personal and moving insight into the emotions and responses experienced demystifies an often-misunderstood disorder.'

— *Alison Matheson, psychotherapist, Oxfordshire Counselling*

'What a pleasure it was to read this honest and heartfelt book. The author writes eloquently about what a struggle being a "borderliner" has been, but importantly makes it possible for a general reader to make a connection, drawing them in with empathy and a degree of understanding. It tells a powerful story very clearly, without self-indulgence (despite being such a personal testimony) and makes for thoughtful and enriching reading.'

— *Ben Ballin, education consultant*

A Sad and Sorry
State of Disorder

of related interest

The Pits and the Pendulum
A Life with Bipolar Disorder
Brian Adams
ISBN 978 1 84310 104 8
eISBN 978 1 84642 358 1

We're All Mad Here
The No-Nonsense Guide to Living with Social Anxiety
Claire Eastham
Foreword by Natasha Devon MBE
ISBN 978 1 78592 082 0
eISBN 978 1 78450 343 7

Hearing Voices, Living Fully
Claire Bien
ISBN 978 1 78592 718 8
eISBN 978 1 78450 322 2

When Anxiety Attacks
Terian Koscik
ISBN 978 1 84819 284 3
eISBN 978 0 85701 232 6

A
Sad *and* Sorry
State *of* Disorder

A Journey into
Borderline Personality Disorder
(and out the other side)

TRACY BARKER

Jessica Kingsley *Publishers*
London and Philadelphia

First published in 2017
by Jessica Kingsley Publishers
73 Collier Street
London N1 9BE, UK
and
400 Market Street, Suite 400
Philadelphia, PA 19106, USA

www.jkp.com

Library of Congress Cataloging in Publication Data
Names: Barker, Tracy, author.
Title: A sad and sorry state of disorder : a journey into borderline
    personality disorder (and out the other side) / Tracy Barker.
Description: London ; Philadelphia : Jessica Kingsley Publishers, 2017.
Identifiers: LCCN 2017001202 (print) | LCCN 2017005778 (ebook) |
ISBN
    9781785923319 (alk. paper) | ISBN 9781784506506 (ebook)
Subjects: LCSH: Borderline personality disorder. | Borderline personality
    disorder--Psychological aspects.
Classification: LCC RC569.5.B67 B36 2017 (print) | LCC RC569.5.B67
(ebook) |
    DDC 616.85/8520651--dc23

British Library Cataloguing in Publication Data
A CIP catalogue record for this book is available from the British Library

ISBN 978 1 78592 331 9
eISBN 978 1 78450 650 6

Printed and bound in the United States

One step – that's all you need
to make it to the next one.
One step, and soon you'll see
how far you've nearly come.

One Step at a Time

Prologue

....

When it was first suggested that I may have a personality disorder, I was deeply insulted. I knew nothing about them at the time, but still I felt as though the fragile essence of who I am was being labelled as entirely wrong.

My indignation was somewhat ironic when I consider that my core belief was exactly this: *'who I am is wrong'*. Perhaps the idea that professionals agreed with this was the cause of my indignation and grievance.

In America, borderline personality disorder used to be known as emotional dysregulation disorder, a label (if one must be labelled) that is wholly more palatable and less disparaging; I also think it is more self-explanatory.

As I began to learn about personality disorders, I discovered that 'borderliners' are commonly referred to as 'heart-sink patients' by many doctors and other professionals; we are a lost cause, with no hope or prospect of recovery or self-improvement. We were, at least, all on the same page. But it did not bode well for me. I already had no hope for myself – the fact that professional bodies generally held the same view was, to say the least, devastating.

To cut a long and tedious story short, it was (after years of toing and froing between one expert and another) recommended that I refer myself to a 'Complex Needs' service in Oxford (who comes up with these names?), the idea being that I was choosing to seek help, rather than being sent against my will.

By now I had been told that Complex Needs was where the no-hopers were sent, because no one else would even try to help us. I had almost given up. I wanted, almost more than anything, to die; the only thing I wanted more was to be okay. Complex Needs was my last chance, and I had to take it. If it didn't work out, I could end my life knowing I had done everything in my power to get better.

The Complex Needs Service in Oxford ran a Therapeutic Community (TC): group therapy on four and a half days a week, for 18 months. It was here that I really began to understand what borderline personality disorder is. I had initially felt condemned by the label, but as I progressed in my therapy, I began to feel empowered by the understanding I was gaining. I was no longer in the dark as to why my emotions, impulses and behaviours were so fierce, extreme and erratic. There was a speck of light at the end of an incredibly long tunnel, and I started to head toward the light with comrades and professionals, who did, actually, believe that there was hope for me.

My diagnosis slowly transformed from a life sentence, into a map by which I could learn to navigate my self, my life and the world around me.

* * * * *

This is not a misery memoir, or a voyeuristic account of how bad it can be to be live with borderline personality disorder. Nor is it a textbook, or a self-help book.

It is me offering hope, if that is what is needed, whether you suffer from borderline personality disorder or care for someone who does.

It is me making an effort to raise awareness of this very misunderstood mental illness.

I am not a professional expert, but I do have experience from the dark side and I have begun to emerge into the light, and I believe that makes me an expert in my own right.

I have been fortunate enough to have had access to a community of peers and facilitators, who supported me, challenged me, believed in me and encouraged me to believe in myself.

I have also been fortunate enough to have a community of friends and family that have believed in me and cared enough to do the same: challenge and support me.

Seeking help was the first of many hurdles I had to overcome, but now, almost seven years after embarking on this journey, I can honestly say that every single difficult, painful and courageous step has been entirely worthwhile.

Throughout the book, I will talk about management rather than recovery, as I believe that management is the first step (after understanding) to recovery. There is no right or wrong way to learn how to manage borderline personality disorder. Nor is there a single magic cure, and no one experience is the same as another. So my journey is just that: my journey.

The poems were written in the depths of borderline episodes; they are raw accounts of the overwhelming despair, distress and turmoil, and they were my attempts, at the time, to make sense of what was happening to me.

This book is an account of my journey of learning to live with borderline, using the National Institute of Mental Health (NIMH) list of symptoms[1] as a guide through the various components that often present in individuals with borderline.

Most importantly, this is an account of how I learned to manage it, and began to recover.

---

1 See www.nimh.nih.gov/health/topics/borderline-personality-disorder/index.shtml#part_145387, accessed on 10 February 2017.

HAUNTED HOUSE

There are phantoms here
roaming free,
making a spectacle of me;
I, who feel them,
sense them,
fear them.
Me. And I alone can see.
Things go missing,
things go wrong,
things go bump;
I, headlong.
Spirits of the undead
live among the dying.
Me, and I alone,
can hear them softly crying.

BORDERLINE

I should know better –
indeed, I do
– but this I cannot control.
I watch events unfold,
a mere spectator,
and yet this is me.
    This is me, whole.
I hear from afar the voice within
and would flee,
myself permitting.
I see from above
the mess I'm in
and sink,
and cannot make me swim.
I know not how it ends,
only that there is no
happily ever after...
So I step back
and let it unfold
because this is me.
    This is me, whole.

Chapter 1

....

For me, this is where it all begins.

Put simply, my sense of self depended largely on other people and how they treated me. If people were nice to me, I believed myself to be nice also – if they weren't nice then nor was I.

I often felt as though the person I was with defined who I was in that moment. When they left, it felt like they had taken 'me' away with them, and I was left floundering, not knowing who I was. I was who they had made me in that instant. That is to say, I existed because they defined me. Without their definition, I was incredibly lost, and I relied on the next interaction to recreate another 'me'. Parallel to this ran a subconscious aim to actually become the person I was with at any given time, be that good or bad, happy or sad, kind or unkind.

In social settings, I would fine-tune my behaviour accordingly. If the occasion was rowdy, I could be rowdy. If it was happy, I could do happy. For me it was like being a social chameleon, which most people can do to some extent. But, as with everything borderline, this was done to the extreme. Not merely to 'fit in' or be acceptable in any given crowd, but to feel like 'someone', and to *become* 'someone'. I wouldn't just show a polite interest in the thoughts and pastimes of those around me, I would embrace them as my own. If I met (and liked) a nurse, I would suddenly want to be a nurse myself, or a security guard, or a bin man and so on. If I spent time with someone who wore nothing but black, I would revamp my entire wardrobe to black. And so it went, and had gone, for many years.

I didn't know who I was or what I wanted. My sense of self was based on who I was with at any given time. So too was my entire sense of being. I tried to become the person or people I was with in order to give some substance and justification to my existence. And I sought desperately to find myself in others by allowing them to define me, or by trying to become someone else.

I had lost myself.

I was lost.

PART OF ME

A part of me
is gone,
crept into the bosom
of your compassion;
I diminish
to give room
to how great
your love could be.
I dissolve
and melt away from me.

A part of me
is gone;
leapt into the embrace
that I imagine.
I depend on you
to keep this
part alive,
and when you don't,
a part of me
is gone.

THICKER THAN WATER

My head's in the clouds,
my feet two feet above the ground –
without doing a thing
you've turned my insides upside down.

Inside-out my crazy world
is melting in my hands,
and ice and fire, and blood and stone
are now my sinking sands.

But you can't get blood from this stone...
or can you –
if you break me down?
If I extinguish all I am
perhaps I'll come around.

I'm skating on the thinnest ice
on the knife-edge blades of my heart –
without saying a word
you've torn my insides all apart.

Back-to-front I've dressed myself
in clothes I'd never wear,
I can't see where I'm headed
running headlong through thin air.

But you can't get blood from this stone...
or can you –
if you break me down?
If I extinguish all of me
perhaps I'll come around.

A STRANGER IN A STRANGER LAND

I don't belong here;
never have, never will –
it is a strange land
and I am stranger still.
I understand their language
but cannot communicate.
I am carried by the crowd,
swallowed in their wake.
I dissolve into the shadows,
sink beneath the strain,
glide across the oddities
for I, too, am strange.
I melt into the background,
enhance the scenery,
but this I know and cannot hide;
there's none so strange as me.

THIS ME

This me is tailor made
to suit your every need –
everything you asked for –
guaranteed to please.
This me is custom built;
designed with you in mind
cleverly constructing
exactly what you want to find.
This me is made to order

created while you wait –
the finest architecture
just as you stipulate.
This me is solely yours
and if you want a change
I'll be happy to accommodate;
I can simply rearrange.

MIRROR, MIRROR

My eyes are not deceived
Truly, this is what I see

A monster;
Seething, clutching
At chances long expired.
A beast;
Heaving, drooling,
Insatiable and wild.
An animal,
Untethered
Wiley, swift and sly.
An alien;
Abnormal, strange,
Come to bleed you dry.

My eyes are not deceived,
This is truly what I see –
Every time I face the mirror
This wretch stares back at me.

So, how did I find myself? My default belief was that I was, essentially, a worthless person. I tried to attribute worth to myself by trying to be someone other than me. The theory is simple: I had to find worth and value within myself, in order to find who I was.

But I also had to find who I was in order to see worth in myself.

The practicalities of this are not so simple. It is an ongoing process that begins with trust. And there we have our first hurdle. It is in the nature of many people with borderline personality disorder to be suspicious and mistrusting, especially when compliments are involved; it is easy to believe it when people criticise us or point out our faults because we know they are telling the truth. I knew I was 'wrong' from the inside out, so I never had a problem with believing someone who backed this up. When I say I didn't have a problem, I don't mean I took it on the chin and it was water off a duck's back – far from it. It hurt like hell and usually resulted in me taking a step further into the mire of self-hatred and self-destruction. But it was easy to believe. It has always been easy to believe.

When people complimented me in any way, I was confused. I wondered why they would say something like that. What was the catch? What did they want? Were they being sarcastic? Were they setting me up to fall? Was it a sick sort of joke?

Because I was confused as to the exact nature of their sinister motives (I was certain this is what they were), my mistrust intensified; here we have a slippery person who is to be avoided at all costs, and if avoiding them is not possible, we need to keep a really close eye on what they're really up to.

I'm not entirely sure how I managed to trust or, rather, how anyone managed to break through my fortified defences. I have had many people tell me I'm good at various things: painting, making jewellery, writing. True enough, I've always enjoyed these things but under my hypercritical eye this has never meant I'm good at them. I assumed therefore that people were merely trying to encourage me to 'distract myself' and do something I like doing.

It was not until I was well into my therapy that these little droplets of affirmation began gradually to soak into my psyche. Combined with learning how to challenge my negative automatic thoughts (NATs) and confronting my intrinsic suspicion, I slowly allowed myself to believe that when someone saw something good in me there might possibly be a grain of truth in it.

I had to begin to trust in the world around me: that it wasn't conspiring against me; that it wasn't out to trip me up and make a fool of me; that there was a small chance that I had (and deserved) a place in the world; that the world was not entirely unsafe.

Hardest of all, I had to begin to trust myself. As I began to find myself, I had to trust what I found, including the weaknesses and flaws that I had to 'own' (God, how I hated that phrase in the Therapeutic Community!) as part of what made me who I am. As I began to discover my own mind, I had to trust in what I thought and felt, as much as I was able to make sense of it in the early days.

As I said, this is an ongoing process, and it is often an uphill struggle. On a bad day, it is all too easy to feel worthless and mistrustful of others and myself, and I can't say I always manage to rise above those feelings. But even that is okay. It's okay to feel low, fed up or even worthless, because these feelings are part of me, and I am (mostly) okay!

Nowadays, a stranger passing me on the street might smile at me because she is a nice person, and I might smile back because I am a nice person too. Or they might not smile because they are in a bad mood, or I might not smile back because I am feeling low, and so on...and that is okay. Because I am learning that who I am is okay.

Chapter 2

Chronic emptiness is a hard state to describe. I was tempted to use the word 'hunger', but that implies that there is something to fill, and that for me was not the case. I was an empty shell, empty, yes – but I did not need filling because what would be the point of filling me? Life had no meaning. I had no purpose.

I wanted to believe there was a meaning to life, but that felt too incongruous to me as I was certain there was no meaning to *me*. How could life mean something, when *my* life doesn't mean anything, when *I* don't mean anything?

I put off getting help for years because I didn't see the point of 'being better'; I couldn't see how being better would give my life a meaning. Also, I was scared that I would get all the help on offer, and there would still be no point to 'me'. Why seek help? *I'm going to die anyway.* Why try to sort my life out? *It's pointless and we'll all die anyway.* Why get better? *There's nothing to get better for.* Don't I want to be happy? *What's the point, it won't last, and I'm going to die one day anyway.*

Chronic emptiness is a black hole within our very fabric – an endless cavern of nothing. I tried to compensate for it in all sorts of ways, but nothing I tried was match enough for the profound emptiness I felt. I tried to be like other people, to give my life some substance-by-proxy, but this only seemed to highlight the extent and depth of the hole. I tried to make myself mean something to other people, make them care for me, but even when I felt cared for the status quo was too tentative to really trust and therefore insufficient to even begin to satiate my core.

It is a deep, intrinsic void subject to rampages of rage, despair, pain, fear, love, joy or hope; sometimes more than one at a time.

It is a hollow, barren, ineffectual state of being.

It is close to hell, I imagine.

BARREN LAND

You will find no signs
of life on my land.
Signs that you trespass,
that you are not welcome,
but no signs to suggest
there is life here.
There will be no fruit
for you to harvest,
and no fruit will come
from what you sow.
My land is barren
but for the shell that is me.

ALL THAT I DO NOT HAVE

All that I do not have,
have not had,
will not know
haunts like a shadow, taunts,
and flaunts its wares
like a temptress,
knowing it is always
beyond my reach;
safe from my desperate grasp,
safe in the knowledge
she need not share
what she has.

WHISPERS OF SOLITUDE

I speak to no one
In particular;
Tales I dare not
Tell a soul.
I sit with someone
I imagine;
Weeping tears
That will not flow.
And all the while
The silence
Insists we do not part.
I whisper to the darkness
And there remains my heart.

IF...

If life was a door, I would close it
If thoughts only dreams, I would wake.
If sleep was an option, I'd choose it
I'll write my own dreams, if I may...

I would leap from the earth
Become weightless and free.
Be a star in the dark
Where you couldn't find me.
Or a storm, or a wave
That you couldn't ignore.
Or maybe an oak tree;
Solid, secure.
Or a bird that could fly
Far, far, far above.
Or the warm rays of sun
You can feel but not touch.

If life was a window I'd smash it
And never look through it again.
I'd find something nicer for building my world;
I'd make it all perfect and then...

THE VERY LAST FALL

I fell –
a long, long fall it was.
I wondered when, if ever,
I would land.

I jumped –
or maybe I was pushed
over the edge of reason –
or was I pulled?

I dropped
like lead into a pit;
a never ending chasm
with no way out.

I died –
but only in a dream –
a dream I had (whilst falling)
that this fall was my last.

ONCE I AM ALIVE

When I stop being dead,
I will live a great life;
once my heart starts to beat
and is no longer ice.

Once I am alive,
I will prove myself wrong;
once my heart starts to beat
and is no longer stone.

When I am born,
I'll be somebody new;
once my heart starts to beat
and is no longer blue.

Once I am alive
you won't recognise me;
once my heart starts to beat...
if my heart starts to beat.

SOUL DESTROYED

Many moons
have lit the road
that these tired feet
have trod.

Many nights
have sat and watched
while this tired mind
sought courage.

Many days
have been amused
by the worn out fears
yet unfounded.

Many souls
have been destroyed
while this one seeks
to fill the void.

One important lesson I had to learn throughout my
therapy is that only I can change things. I couldn't keep
waiting for somebody else to give meaning to my life, or
purpose, or direction.

It took a lot of hard work (not just by myself I might add) to begin to emerge from this state of futility. I had to work through the stages of my life that had brought me to where I was, and I had to dare to trust people who told me they believed in me – no mean feat for a person with borderline, and no mean feat for the people who kept believing, and kept telling me this, despite the fact that to literally hit their head against a brick wall may well have been less painful.

Each time I challenged my default belief that I was worthless I took a step closer to believing for myself. My sense of self had to become less dependent on others, which meant I had to learn to accept what I saw in myself, for myself. I had to accept my limitations and my failures as part of what made me. I had to be my own friend, my own rescuer, and a believer in myself. I speak in past tense as if the job is done when, in reality, there is still a fraction of a void that needs my attention.

Taking responsibility for myself was key in all of this 'self-management' and 'road to recovery'.

Anyone who suffers from these feelings of chronic emptiness will know that none of these steps are one-off steps. Nothing happens overnight – literally nothing. It is a slow chipping away (or in this case filling) which takes blood, sweat and tears alongside constant setbacks, relentless self-doubt and endless second-guessing and soul-searching (searching first for the soul, and then searching the contents of the newly discovered soul).

It is accepting that *you are*. And then accepting that you are *who you are*, whether you like it or not.

It is believing, as much as you dare, that you can be someone just by being.

It is bloody hard work.

Chapter 3

....

Having stress-related paranoid thoughts
Having severe dissociative symptoms, such as feeling cut off from oneself,
observing oneself from outside the body, or losing touch with reality

Studies show that people with this disorder may see anger in an
emotionally neutral face and have a stronger reaction to words with
negative meanings than people who do not have the disorder.

(NIMH)

I have heard this paranoia described as 'unrealistically
self-conscious', but I hardly think it is at all unrealistic,
given that my position in the world around me is
determined by other people: whether they are kind or
unkind, and whether they are kind or unkind to me.
Considering the void and sense of meaninglessness at
the core of my (non)being, it is understandable I think,
why my paranoid ideation might be so prevalent. It may
be irrational, but I don't think it is unrealistic.

Being conscious of myself in relation to others, and
how they viewed me, was essential for my existence. I
didn't want to appear stupid, wrong or irritating. I was
constantly on the lookout for signals – body language,
eye-rolls, subtle comments – that would alert me to how
irritating I was being. And I found them everywhere
I looked. My shrewd (but warped) observations of the
reactions of those around me confirmed my fears that

I was, indeed, a source of great irritation and that *I* was wrong.

You could say I saw what I wanted to see, though why I would want to see that the world is full of disdain or, at best, indifference towards me I cannot say. Perhaps it was part of substantiating my tentative hold on 'me' – I am a nuisance, a blight on the landscape of life, and I needed to see that others felt *something* about me in order to feel validated as a human being. As I said: warped.

But the fact remains that what people thought of me determined who I was. For me, episodes of paranoia were frequent, and as a result the threat of abandonment – be it real or imagined – was constantly imminent in my mind; I was certain I was going to be rejected in the next few minutes, every minute of my life.

These episodes intensified alarmingly in response to what I perceived as *actual* abandonment (as opposed to a mere threat). My paranoia would accelerate from routine background checks to a full state of emergency in a matter of seconds. I knew what people were thinking, I just *knew*; I had been abandoned and it felt like annihilation. There was no point in me speaking to the person who was spiking the particular surge as I could already narrate what they would say to me: because I knew. I was adamant, and I was right. And I was terrified.

THE EYES

Don't be deceived by the eyes –
the kindest, gentlest eyes –
behind which lies
a cold, biting malice;
indifference with a twist.
And yet...
   and yet...
they truly are
the most gentle eyes
I ever fell into.
Left for dead,
the latest victim
of the killer eyes' sting –
piercing and plucking the heart
as they turned away;
oblivion, with a twist.
And yet...
   oh yes...
they truly are
the most beautiful eyes
if I really must die.

And then, the after-life:
eternity spent gazing into the eyes
long since closed to me. And
in time the malice is forgotten –
the sting, still keen, but forgiven.
And so in death itself I am
once more deceived by the eyes –
the kindest,
most gentle eyes
I ever fell into.

I'VE COME TO DISAPPOINT YOU

I read your face and see
All you do not say;
The lines of disappointment
Etched around your eyes,
The unmet expectations
That hide behind your smile.
The lack of comprehension
When I fail to overcome,
The questions you don't ask
About the things I have not done.
The pain, because I've let you down
And, no doubt will again.
The fear that I may never be
The way I was back then.

REMAINS OF THE DAY

Small though they are
I feverishly collect each moment;
remnants to relive
when it's all over.
A little kindness here,
a gentle touch there,
the odd smile and
understanding sigh.
And once all is said and done,
nothing. But a fabrication
of reality –
A phantom feast of love lost.
But love was never born.

RUMOURS OF LOVE

Whispered words
pad softly down deserted corridors.
Silent wishes flutter
    unuttered
        through a hole
that used not – ought not – to be there;
they, at least, go free.
Rumours of love
echo carelessly,
sending ripples of hope
across stagnant waters.
Rumours of love…
    drowned
        by a shudder of despair.

FURTHER

But, this time, further
than ever before.
Before it happened
we saw the fall.
    And from afar
    we watched us
    walk, serenely.
And in the distance
we heard
our whispered voices;
a dull, compelling beat,
a flat, hypnotic drone:
    "you ought to go,

> you need to go,
> you have to go".
> And so we go
> further than before.
> And, lurking in the shadows,
> we sit and watch the fall.

Oddly, and contrary to my firm belief at the time, life did not revolve around me. One of the many contradictions in a borderliner: we are worthless, meaningless, unlovable, and yet we believe that other people are spending their energies and emotions on deliberately belittling or hurting us.

With my desperate search to mean something, and my equally desperate need for somebody else to give me that validation, it is somewhat understandable that I inexorably saw myself through their eyes (and remember; I was *always* right about what they were thinking).

But what if – just *if* – they weren't 'looking' at me at all? Just suppose that I was wrong to believe I was seeing myself through their eyes. Maybe they were my eyes all along, imagining what they must be seeing, and assuming they were thinking the same as me. This was an absurd alternative reality when first posited to me, but one which opened up a whole new – and frightening – world.

Maybe Sasha looked pissed off when I passed her in the doorway, not because she was irritated by my presence, but because she'd just dropped her car key down a drain. Maybe Anna ignored me, not because she can't stand the sight of me and pretended I wasn't there, but because she was thinking about her sick mother. Maybe Lizzie didn't answer her phone not because she saw it was me calling and couldn't stand to talk to me, but because she was answering the door to the postman. Maybe the doctor didn't rush through my appointment because she was sick to the back teeth of me, but because she was coming to the end of a very long day.

Seriously? It's that straightforward? Again, the theory is but the practicalities are laborious, monotonous and tedious. Numerous potholes line the road of freedom from 'paranoid ideation', and although they are spread out more now, they are still there, and I still fall into them. This is not a fight I can ever imagine winning completely, but as I persevere in acknowledging that my perceptions are warped, and my paranoia is unwarranted, I win more battles than I lose.

I get up quicker than I used to and I move on more easily, despite how wearisome it can be to constantly feel as though I'm at war against the machinations of my own mind. I am constantly attempting to re-wire my brain and shift the gears of thinking that are so instinctive and unrelenting.

As I continue to challenge my perspective of what is happening, my intrinsic suspicion and paranoia is gradually becoming more subdued and less potent. It is a very gradual process, and it is thoroughly exhausting.

Chapter 4

A pattern of intense and stormy relationships with family, friends, and loved ones, often veering from extreme closeness and love (idealization) to extreme dislike or anger (devaluation)

This is all about a tendency towards an 'all or nothing' mentality. There is only love or hate, which is based on this or that whim and suspicion (and the conviction that the world is, essentially, against me). Everything is black or white, and everything is extreme. Without wanting to over-simplify this incredibly complicated status quo, it seems obvious to me why I was capable of both extreme idealisation and devaluation often within a matter of minutes: if someone is nice to me, I feel like a nice person; if they are not *quite* as nice on another occasion (believe me when I say the margin here is infinitesimal) I feel like the most atrocious person ever to walk the earth.

Who I was did not depend on me, it depended on other people and how they were towards me. When Diane smiled at me on Monday, I thought she was the most wonderful person at the Therapeutic Community; I spent the day craving her approval and affirmation, trying to make eye contact with her to ensure that I was still okay. When she walked past me on Wednesday and didn't even look in my direction, I hated everything about her (and I mean everything), and I spent that day feeling resentful, suspicious and angry. Why? Because one day I was a good person, and the next I was not, and this was all Diane's fault. This was how I saw the world, and my own worth.

I was too hyper-vigilant for my own good; I clocked and scrutinised every single word and facial expression of anyone I had contact with. My opinion of myself would change more often than I imagine the whole population of London has eaten hot dinners, and so too did my opinion of others.

If Lizzie used the adjective 'lovely' to describe something I had done and the next time used 'nice', I would instantly feel less of a person. I would frantically try to work out what I had done wrong to go from lovely to nice. Because the precise words Lizzie used, the body language of my GP, the facial expression of the bus driver – all told me whether I was good or bad, right or wrong. It also affected how I felt towards the other person – I would either love them, or hate them.

There is only black and white; there is no grey. Things (and people) are either all good or all bad with no in between, and I was no exception. The blacks and the whites are always extreme and painfully intense. With no middle ground, no balance, it is hardly surprising that borderline sufferers are so unstable, volatile and seemingly impossible to reason with. Perhaps this is why doctors refer to us as 'heart-sink patients'!

I LOVE YOU — IS THAT OKAY?

I hope you don't mind
that I love you
if it's easier
I won't tell a soul.
If you prefer
I won't even tell you,
so that only myself
ever knows.

I hope you're not scared
that I love you –
if you are
I won't let you see.
If you'd rather
I'll keep it a secret inside
which will hurt,
but will only hurt me.

WHERE I BEGIN

I begin here:
where I disappear
into your kindness
long after it is spent.
I begin now
and end, somehow,
all at once
because, yesterday, you cared.

I begin soon
returning to the womb
of a heart that almost loves me
but not quite.
I begin
when you breathe life into me.
I begin
when I'm in your arms.
But I end
the moment you release me
and love and hate
and hope and truth
begin, then, to devour me.

MOCKING BIRD

You weep, and yet
you do not learn.
You leap into the fire
knowing it will burn.
You laugh your hollow,
empty laugh
and, horrified, I watch the crash:
a slow-motion repeat
of tragedy and gore;
a paused, rewound catastrophe,
as all the times before.
You run, but you
can never hide;
the demons are alive and well
inside.

Your cry for help
will not be heard
above the cackle of
the mocking bird.

ANOTHER DAY, ANOTHER FALL

Another day, I have no choice
I can't ignore compulsion's voice
Convincing lies that twist the truth
And strangle
Each last beauty.

Another fall, I carry on
Vain repetition of a tuneless song
Words that silence every hope
And steal the joy
And kill the soul.

Another fight I didn't win
One reason more to just give in
The myth of victory holds on
Until my life,
And body's gone.

This is where I needed to introduce some grey: I had to
entertain the possibility that there could be something
other than black. Or white. I had to accept that good
and bad can co-exist in a person, or situation, and that
this was okay.

A nice person can be in a bad mood. A kind person can ignore you. An unkind person can smile at you. A bad person might help you if you were in need. Basically, an isolated act of any individual does not make them all good, or all bad.

I don't think I began to engage this way of thinking until I had left the Therapeutic Community. I suspect it was easier to practise with one person at a time, rather than a room of more than 20 people.

The Therapeutic Community taught me basic boundary ground rules: what was acceptable behaviour; what was a good alternative to unacceptable behaviour; what were reasonable expectations and what were unreasonable demands; where somebody else ended, and where I began; where I ended, and where somebody else began; what was my shit to deal with, and what was not mine at all.

With one person at any given time I found it much easier to bear all these rules in mind, and to pick my way through them one at a time. In the Therapeutic Community I had gradually managed to be marginally less impulsive, to the extent that sometimes I had almost a full second standing between me and an explosion. These were the most crucial seconds out of my whole 18 months in therapy. They offered a pause to think, breathe, calm down, challenge my certainty of what was happening and rustle up a way to handle how I felt without an implosion or explosion. All this in less than a second.

In the early days, my attempts to master this daunting feat were along the lines of blurting out:

'you've really *seriously* pissed me off' (perhaps not quite so politely), and then holding my breath waiting for an equally angry comeback. Oddly, people seemed quite proud of my newfound communication skills! The fact that I had said how I felt, albeit abruptly and clumsily, was a genuine accomplishment. Rather than storming out, or sitting silently while scraping skin off my hand with my fingernail, or scribbling what I was thinking in my notebook, I laid the ground for a conversation.

I was fortunate to have the safety of the Therapeutic Community in which to explore my macabre alternative behaviours. They were crude, but they were alternative, and my peers and facilitators recognised them for what they were: growth and the tentative first steps of self-management and accepting responsibility for how I feel.

An important stage in the process of managing these extreme and intense emotions was to learn not to run away from them. As I dared to stay with the feelings, I was able to start identifying *what* the feelings actually were, and more importantly *why* they were. The more I was able to pause and not instantly explode, the more I was able to accept the feelings. The feelings were slightly more acceptable with the immediate threat of a complete meltdown removed (even if only temporarily) from the equation, but still they were often uncomfortable and painful, and always extreme.

I am pleased to say that my pauses now last far longer than almost a second, and my resulting response is generally more palatable. I use the precious seconds of pauses that I have to work out as much as I can about what is happening for me, and – if I have any spare time – what is happening for 'them'. I hurtle through my acceptable options of how to respond and deal with what I am feeling, and more often than not I choose a reasonable option.

I do my best to take responsibility for myself; to consider how I have contributed to what I am feeling and not blame others if my perception is warped. I flit through my expectations and understanding of the present boundaries, and I aim to accept what is mine (and me) and what is not. I try to remember, while I pause, that good and bad can coexist; that people are imperfect and that is okay. I am imperfect and that is okay too.

It is an art that I am still fine-tuning. Those vital seconds present me with the opportunity to take back control from the impulsivity and extremes that are the hallmark of borderline. They give me the space to squint and see grey. They are only seconds, but they have saved me (and probably others) hours, and days, of turmoil and misery and destruction.

Never underestimate the power of the pause. For so many it is a natural process that occurs probably without conscious thought or effort. But for those of us who have to work at it, it is a phenomenal and powerful achievement.

Chapter 5

Frantic efforts to avoid real or imagined abandonment

Seemingly mundane events may trigger symptoms. For example, people with BPD may feel angry and distressed over minor separations—such as vacations, business trips, or sudden changes of plans—from people to whom they feel close.

(NIMH)

'If a tree falls in a forest and no one is around to hear it, does it make a sound?'

If my existence depends on certain 'others' and they are not around to validate my existence, do I exist at all?

In the Therapeutic Community we faced devastating desertions and abandonments pretty much on a daily basis. Whether it was a peer leaving after their 18 months, a staff member who was absent (I swear the staff would absent themselves sometimes just to give us extra practice at facing up to our issues), a peer who was off sick, or a staff member running late, there were always inevitable meltdowns.

Feelings ranged from resentment, panic, anger (verging on feeling livid), more panic and, deep, overwhelming distress. It didn't matter if the abandonment was only in my imagination; it was absolutely real to me and nobody could convince me otherwise.

Our environment defines us. It validates us or negates us, accepts us or rejects us, loves or hates us, affirms us or crushes us. That being the case, it is no wonder that I was overwhelmed by what is sometimes referred to as 'intense fear and inappropriate anger', when my source of definition was nowhere to be found, or was leaving early, or was leaving on time but leaving nonetheless.

It might be worth noting at this point, that to me abandonment and rejection was one and the same thing, and it was *always* personal. If I didn't get a job I applied for, it was personal. If a driver didn't let me out of a side road, it was personal. If a magazine didn't publish a poem, it was personal. All of these miscreants and more had a personal vendetta against me. They didn't like *me*. It didn't matter how many times people told me that 'it's nothing personal'; to me, rejection and abandonment always has been and always will be personal.

Unlike some with borderline personality disorder, I was not intolerant to being alone – on the contrary – I was more than happy to be alone. But when I was *supposed* to be with someone and there was a glitch in the proceedings (from that someone being five minutes late, to the time coming to a natural end) I was wholly intolerant; in that moment I absolutely could not cope with being 'alone'.

The panic and anger were equal in force, and both were equally uncontrollable. If I cried, it was hard to work out whether it was due to hurt, anger or fear.

When I hurt myself I didn't know whether I was trying to cull the rage, dull the pain or stall the panic.

In the face of any form of abandonment, the only thinking I did was how to stop the pain. For years, I succumbed to a myriad of extreme and agonising emotions, and my primitive fight or flight brain attempted to alleviate these emotions any way it could.

WHAT IS LEFT

A cold chill that numbs the senses,
a silence that suffocates,
an age-old emptiness filled anew,
and a sea of truths and lies
so vast and dark and deep
that each becomes the other.

A quiet rage that stops the heart,
a hunger that is starved,
a shadow that does not belong
and a river of flesh and blood
so fast and strong and steep
that its boundaries are no more.

A wreck that keeps on wrecking,
a pain that causes more,
a loneliness that crowds itself,
and a well of shame and dread
so infinite and bleak
that to drown would be a mercy.

But mercy is not
what is left.

HOLD ME BACK

I don't exactly
want to break my fall,
for then you would not know
I fell apart.
Nor do I, though,
wish to fall apart
without you here – and you,
believing I can stand,
would make me.
I do not want
you thinking I am happy
and yet I neither want
you sad that I am not.
I'd like that we
could both still share
our time and space,
and know
that each still knows
the other.

GIVE ME A BREAK

So very nearly fixed
And then you wreck it all again.
Almost the final stitch,
But you pull the hanging thread.
Not far from back together
When you rip it all apart.
So close to being whole,
And again, you break my heart.

JUST FOR YOU

This is what I had for you:
What you wouldn't take
And this is what I still have now,
But now is far too late.

I have a well of love inside
A love I can't express
I can't find words to let it out
It gives no peace, no rest.

I think it was meant just for you
Although you wouldn't take it
And nobody can fill the void
And nothing can replace it.

It sits in me, it tortures me,
It wants to hold and lavish
It destroys the ones it wants so much
It cannot find its place.

I hate this love, I wish it dead
I curse the pain it causes.
I curse the hearts that turned away
And made this love an orphan.

GOODBYE

I will avert my gaze,
Pretend I didn't see you
Look away.
I will stumble through
The awkward silence
So as to relieve you.
I will not linger
Despite myself,
Nor wait for you
To catch yourself.
I'll do all I can
To reassure you
And convince you
I'm just fine.
And this, so well,
That for a second
I, too, believe
That I don't mind.

In all honesty, I can't tell you how I have learnt to
manage these irrational feelings of abandonment and
rejection; I don't think I have.

I still experience a flutter of panic when I can't
get hold of my best friend, Lizzie, and I find myself
wracking my brains to work out what I might have done
to upset her. I have to remind myself that Lizzie has
stood by me through thick and thin for years, and she is
not likely to desert me now.

I still have to convince myself that my wife, Dawn, really does love me when she's stuck at work and two hours late home (who am I kidding; half an hour late will do it). Or when she's left me in bed on a Saturday morning and taken the dogs out without me. I mean seriously, who wouldn't be delighted at the gift of a dog-free Saturday morning lie in? But I need to have stern conversations with myself and summon to mind every piece of evidence I can, to tentatively trust that she has not left the house because she can't bear the sight of me any more.

What I have learned to manage is how I deal with the panic. On the whole I manage not to hurt myself. I might still cry, throw things and sometimes scream with rage, but I have also learned that this is my shit and not my wife's. Fortunately for Dawn, I don't take my panic out on her and, as is often the nature of a borderliner, the minute she comes home all rage and panic and hurt are forgotten and forgiven.

I am fortunate to have a wife who understands how this works for me, and who supports me completely. She no longer promises to be home at a certain time if she cannot guarantee it; she even adds 30 minutes onto her expected time home to allow for unforeseen hold ups. She does not tiptoe around me, however, and this is important for both of us. I need to learn to strengthen my internal dialogue that helps me challenge the voice of panic, and Dawn needs to be able to be herself without constantly being afraid of doing something that may result in a meltdown.

Dawn is not my rescuer; this boundary was set firmly in place the minute we got together. She supports me, loves me, understands me, and if I ask her to, she will help me. But she will never rescue me, and I do not want her to. This is a vital parameter; not only for mine and Dawn's relationship, but for all other relationships and friendships I have including my relationship with myself.

It is important for me to apply these same principles whenever I feel the threat of panic arising from the sense of abandonment; I have to rescue myself, and not force that responsibility onto anyone else. I must question my beliefs and perspectives and read in-between the lines of my habitual assumptions that I am 'wrong' and therefore abandonment is imminent.

I once attended a conference about Therapeutic Communities, and the speaker posited the idea that a sense of belonging is crucial for the recovery (or, at the very least, the management) of borderline personality disorder. This is a theory in which I am a firm believer, and it is a strong endorsement for the principle of 18 months in a Therapeutic Community (where each member belongs, and has sufficient time to recognise and trust this inclusion). My most intense feelings of abandonment or rejection have occurred when I have felt I do not belong.

With the luxury of belonging I am feeling less and less this debilitating, panic-induced paralysis of abandonment, but I still experience moments where I have to work damn hard not to give in to what absolutely is (but clearly isn't) abandonment.

Chapter 6

Inappropriate, intense anger or problems controlling anger

The full force of my anger was mostly expressed when I was alone, and was largely taken out on myself. There were times in the Therapeutic Community (and elsewhere) when I did express my anger publicly, and often with biting sarcasm. But physically it was I that bore the brunt of my anger (if we ignore, for example, the odd chair or door that I kicked in passing).

It is hard to say where the anger actually comes from, but I would suspect it stems from a lack of control; certainly in my case I think this is more than likely. I had no control over other people, or circumstances (such as a bus being late, a phone call I was expecting doesn't materialise, the exact pizza I had set out to buy is not in stock...the list is endless). More importantly, perhaps, I had no control over myself or my feelings.

It is like opening the door of a hot oven, with your head almost in it ready to look inside. The blast of the heat is stifling – it hits your eyes, and for a minute you can't see properly, and it floods your lungs and you feel suffocated by the shock. The oven door is, however, a door in my conscious thought, and the heat was an unforeseen glitch in how I was expecting, or needing, things to go.

The overwhelming fear I experienced prior to a daunting situation would result in intense feelings of frustration and anger. I often felt angry with myself for not being able to cope with life like a 'normal' person. I felt angry because I was so weak and afraid, and I felt angry because I didn't understand why I couldn't just live my life like everyone else seemingly managed to do.

I would berate myself mercilessly following every panic attack or episode of self-mutilation, and I was sadly unaware that this self-condemnation only served to further intensify the initial feelings.

People with borderline personality disorder have been described as having no emotional skin. The emotions we experience are the same as those of any other person, but the intensity and extreme of emotion is where we differ. We don't feel disappointment, we feel devastation. We don't get annoyed, we get livid. We don't feel sad, we feel utter despair. Nor do we feel pleased about something; we feel beside ourselves with excitement. If we are happy we could conquer the world, in that moment. It is as though there is no filter to dilute the normal, everyday emotions that are an unavoidable part of life.

And so it is with anger – a frenzy of extreme and excessive fury which, more often than not, is highly inappropriate.

ANGER

It's in there somewhere;
a monster in my belly.
Sometimes I feel it shifting,
or sense its muffled yelling.
It's big, ugly, scary;
uncontrollable.
It's hidden well, I like to think,
and doesn't cause much trouble.
It's right there – I know it;
a monster in my head –
some days I feel it fighting
or, so still it could be dead.
But it doesn't die,
it doesn't rest –
it roars and screams and shouts.
It beats me up in every way
and I'm scared to let it out.

DON'T YOU DARE

Don't make me talk
just because you can.
Don't make me tell you things
if you don't give a damn.
Don't make me feel bad
if I tell you I can't.
Don't make me feel wrong
when it all falls apart.
Don't make me feel things

that you can't take away.
Don't tell me to trust you
if you're not here to stay.

ONE OF US DIES

The heart swells with hope;
Swells to bursting,
And it does.
No more an instrument
Of life
But of destruction –
A carrier of poison
And ruin.
And the beating
Turns to thumping,
Turns to bleeding,
And then...
Silence.
    'Til something beats no more
And one of us dies.

In order to gain control, I had to learn to stand back
from the oven door, but before I could learn this I had
to discover what triggered the opening of the door.
Unfortunately for me, this was practically everything.
    If not understanding myself was a main player
in this cycle repeating itself, is stands to reason that

understanding would be equally key in breaking the cycle. As with all of the steps of self-discovery and self-management, this is much easier said than done.

I confess I am guilty of using and abusing one of the first steps of helping to control these outbursts; mainly, that I avoid the 'triggers' and situations where I know they will be at large. When practically everything triggers the anger, this means an awful lot of avoidance.

That was quite a confession.

However, there are some things even I can't avoid, and I usually manage reasonably well to navigate a way through these.

One of the banes of my life in the Therapeutic Community was 'thought diaries' – how I hated them with vengeance. However, as much as I hate to admit it, they have actually proved helpful (years down the line). I haven't actually completed a thought diary since the Therapeutic Community, but the principle of them has stayed with me and oh, so very slowly I have learned to apply the basic concept in my life.

A thought diary is a breakdown of scenarios of a particular situation that is destined to prove problematic. Once identifying the problem, you work through the worst-case scenario, including the worst possible consequences. Then, you consider how you might circumnavigate the problem, so that the worst-case scenario can be avoided, or at least lessened in impact. You also explore the potential consequences of a successful circumnavigation, considering what might, actually, go to plan, and how that would feel. The last stage of the dreaded diary is to reflect on what *actually* happened (yes, they made us face the fear and do it anyway). We then had to describe how we felt about what happened, and how we could do it differently next time.

I think the idea behind the thought diaries was to challenge our worst fears by facing them head-on, the hope being that we would look back at our completed diary and realise that they were unfounded, and that the worst-case scenario was nowhere near as drastic as our initial predictions.

I cannot put my hand on my heart and say in all honesty that I took these exercises in the least bit seriously, or that I put a single ounce of my heart or soul into them. I considered thought diaries to be a complete waste of time and paper. I admit I was afraid; what if I tried my hardest to take back control, to try and avoid a meltdown and the subsequent outburst, and what if I failed? And what if, next time, I tried to circumnavigate a problem, and still failed? So I didn't try. I filled in my diaries with a self-defeating contempt; I was adamant 'it' would be as bad as I feared, and I made no effort whatsoever to prove myself wrong.

Clearly, the thought diaries made enough of an impression on me that I still remember them, and the idea behind them (albeit none too fondly). It really *is* about feeling the fear and doing it anyway. Not, as I thought at the time, about finding a way to feel no fear at all.

For more years than I care to remember, I was fear personified. The worst that could happen would usually be that I would fail to be in control of myself, my feelings and my surroundings. This invariably resulted in a self-destructive implosion which could last for days, depending on the magnitude of the catastrophe.

I can't recall the first time I trusted in this process of alternative scenarios, but I am glad I at least felt strongly enough about the futility of thought diaries to memorise their pointless steps. Enough to eventually wonder, what if – just *if* – I could understand my fear of the situation: would there then be a way forward to (gasp) an alternative scenario?

None of the individual lessons learnt along my journey of management of borderline are isolated or independent of the others. To understand the fear I had to understand the roots, and to do that I had to understand myself, and to do that I had to continue on my quest to find myself.

Chapter 7

....

Recurring suicidal behaviors or threats or self-harming behavior, such as
*   cutting*

Self-injurious behavior includes suicide and suicide attempts, as well
as self-harming behaviors, described below. As many as 80 percent
of people with BPD have suicidal behaviors, and about 4 to 9 percent
commit suicide.

*   Unlike suicide attempts, self-harming behaviors do not stem from*
a desire to die. However, some self-harming behaviors may be life
threatening. Self-harming behaviors linked with BPD include cutting,
burning, hitting, head banging, hair pulling, and other harmful acts.
People with BPD may self-harm to help regulate their emotions, to
punish themselves, or to express their pain. They do not always see these
behaviors as harmful.

(NIMH)[2]

These behaviours are sometimes referred to as 'self-
mutilating behaviours'. I have to say, I hate the term
'self-mutilation', and much prefer 'self-harm' (if one
can prefer any such description). However, I think it
is important to call a spade a spade: I mutilated myself.
Yes, I hurt my body, but ultimately it was a mutilation
of everything I was.

....

2   NIMH (2013) *Borderline Personality Disorder.* NIH Publication No. 11-4928.
    Washington, DC: U.S. Department of Health and Human Services.

For me, I don't think my self-mutilating behaviour was as much to do with reaffirming an ability to feel as it was with trying to understand *what* I was feeling. It is hard to explain to somebody (self included) what you feel, when you feel so much at once, out of the blue, at such extremes and with such fierce intensity. For me it was also a desperate act of self-preservation.

Whenever I was aware that the pressure within was building to a dangerous crescendo, I was terrified of the potential consequences should that crescendo be reached. It was essential to relieve some pressure and, at the same time, shift the focus from within to without. My inner turmoil took a back seat as I was forced to attend to the more pressing external problem I had just created. I would even posit that this was my primitive way of trying to 'pause' – I was aware that I was losing control, and this was a crude attempt to take it back.

When the pain became physical I believed that I understood what I was feeling, although I still didn't understand it enough to put into words at the time. The emotional pain became embodied in the tangible, physical (and usually) visible pain; by seeing how I felt, I could almost begin to understand it. I also believed that now there was a physical manifestation of my distress, it would be easier for others to understand it, though I suspect now that it merely served to add to the confusion and misunderstanding of what on earth was going on.

Sometimes the act of self-mutilation was a conscious attempt to still the storm within, and sometimes it was much more impulsive. There were other times when my self-mutilation was an act of self-sabotage. This was not usually a cognitive process, but a process nonetheless whereby I would hurt myself in order to sabotage any illusion of improvement. I was certain that people would expect me to continue improving, and I was terrified that any improvement I may have made was not sustainable. I understand now that I was trying to invalidate peoples' expectations of me, because I was afraid I would never be able to live up to even the smallest of them.

At the time, self-mutilation helped me, and it had helped for years. It was a primitive grounding technique which also, ironically, kept me alive.

Because I felt my life was so pointless and meaningless, the desire to end it all was constant. I had a safety net; I knew that if things got too bad there was always suicide. And in the interim, for situations that didn't quite warrant that drastic step, I would mutilate my poor, innocent body.

I had spent many years surviving what were, for me, excruciating ordeals, by telling myself: *it's okay, you can kill yourself when this is over.*

For many years I lived (a pitiful half-life, but yes I lived) with a constant desire not to be here. The background track in my psyche was *I wish I was dead*. If things were hard, scary, confusing, painful, I wished I was dead. I even wished I was dead when I was happy because I knew it wouldn't last, so what was the point of feeling it at all?

I wish I was dead had become my mantra. All day, every day, I wished I was dead, and my security blanket was that I could act on the thought any time I chose.

There were many other times where I absolutely *needed* to die: I didn't *wish* I was *dead*, I *wanted* to *die*. There is a fine distinction between the two. One is a terribly negative and painful way to begrudgingly exist; the other is potentially catastrophic.

Like all of the symptoms and criteria of borderline personality disorder I do not believe there is a 'one size fits all' rule, and from one individual to the next there may be several different reasons why self-mutilation is so habitual. I still struggle to explain how it helped me, because I don't fully understand myself, with hindsight, how abusing myself could possibly serve to enable me to survive. But it did.

I don't think it necessary to explore the precise ins-and-outs of this criterion, nor do I think it would be helpful. Suffice to say these behaviours only serve to perpetuate an already impossible status quo, despite being our only apparent resource in the moment of crisis.

THE END

I see no end
therefore I crave one.
An end, to end
the endlessness of failing;
an end, to break
the never-ending fall.
An end, to end
the fear of never knowing
the end.

SELF-DESTRUCT

This is how we stop the pain.
This is how we feel again;
feel real,
feel alive,
feel as though we haven't died.
This is how we make us matter
if only to ourselves;
make us count,
make us mean
something, make us feel seen.
This is how we start again.
This is how we forget pain;
forget mistakes,
forget we care,
forget: we have a new nightmare.
This is how we know
we haven't died.

STRANGE ENCHANTMENTS

Soon we will go, I can sense it
down to the solemn abyss,
where memories prey on the present no more
and all is in silence but this:
    The thud of our footsteps
    parading the past,
    the scream
    that is lost in the dark,
    the thump of our heart
    beating cold prison walls,
    the breath that we stole
    as our last.

And soon we will fall, I can feel it;
the impulse of life, now so faint.
The drag of the tide creeping out from the shore
sweeps us away as we wait.

TALKING TO MYSELF

If they won't listen
I will not speak
At least, not out loud.
If they don't care
I won't let on
Well, not so they can see.

I shall tell myself
In my secret language,

I will etch it in my flesh.
And I'll use this pain
To take away
The pain I can't express.
I will tear apart
The life that's left
And watch it waste away.
And every wound will spell a word
You would not let me say.

NICE TRY

You're trying hard
To kill me
And although I'm on your side
I will fight you
When you get too close
In case I change my mind.
And your efforts
To destroy me,
While valiant, are mad;
For how could you
Annihilate
A life I have not had.

SURVIVAL OF THE WEAK

I survive
but I do not overcome.
I go on living
but I die.
I manage
but I really do not cope.
I go on smiling
while I cry.

I survive,
but it isn't quite enough.
I fight the fight
to no avail.
I endure
but I do not persevere.
I try my best,
but I fail.

Again, there is no quick-fix for overcoming the urges
and impulses that come so naturally, and seem (at
the time) to serve an invaluable purpose. The path to
managing these behaviours is long (*seriously* long), all
uphill and riddled with one step forward followed by
two steps back.

Sometimes managing to resist the impulse is a
case of sheer willpower; at other times it is a matter of
believing in myself. But as with all the stages of self-
management, and learning to regulate our emotions,
it is intertwined with the process of understanding

ourselves, finding ourselves and slowly adjusting our perspective of the world and those in it.

It is also a massively uncomfortable dose of taking responsibility for ourselves, and an equally large and terrifying measure of believing things can be different, and that life can get better.

After each of my failed attempts to take my own life there was a deep sense of frustration and failure. Once this had passed, however, eventually there came a confusing sense of relief in the fact that I had failed.

Although I constantly wished I was dead (ignoring the times that I *needed* to be dead), there was clearly a part of me, spectacularly hidden, that did not wish to die. I had to acknowledge this part and learn to listen to it.

I remember at least two professionals asking me: why, if I so desperately wanted to die, had I not killed myself yet? The temptation to interpret this as a challenge was enormous, as was the temptation to assume they, too, wanted me dead. Perhaps they were simply trying to encourage me to search for the hidden fragment within myself that did not, actually, wish to die?

I had already learned, without even trying, that these feelings of *needing* to die eventually passed. I began to tell myself before the crisis reached a climax that, *this too shall pass,* and after months (if not years) of resisting the urge to act upon my suicidal feelings I began to actually believe it: *this too shall pass,* and it always did.

Once I believed this, I began to apply it to the other urges and impulses of self-mutilation. I utilised the power of the pause to remind myself that the intensity of my emotions would not be unbearable forever. *This too shall pass.*

It has taken much practice and determination to swap one mantra for another, but I have done it, and it is no longer a bloody battle to summon the new mantra to the front of my mind when I need it.

It has become my new life-line: *This too shall pass.*

Chapter 8

....

Impulsive and often dangerous behaviors, such as spending sprees, unsafe sex, substance abuse, reckless driving, and binge eating

Quite frankly, does it matter if I don't have money for rent and I get evicted? *I can just kill myself.* What does it matter if I spend all my rent money on binge-food, or new clothes in an attempt to reinvent myself every day? *I can kill myself when it all goes belly up.*

I can't honestly say that my self-damaging behaviours were thought through with such clarity, but when my bank balance was dangerously depleted, I did have my trusty safety net to bail me out: I could kill myself if I needed to.

I had no boundaries, and I had no direction. I was depressed, frightened, lonely, uncomfortable in my own skin, and I had no respect for myself or my life, because I saw no point in myself. There was never any hope that I could be 'better' so why not just finish a bad job?

I took no responsibility for myself whatsoever. It was not my fault, not my choice; I couldn't help it. For many years it did not occur to me that I could (or should) assume responsibility for myself and my actions. I didn't blame other people, but nor did I blame myself that my life was such a pitiful mess. I absolved myself completely from any guilt and responsibility. It was just how I was, and I couldn't help it.

I was reckless because nothing mattered, myself included. I was irresponsible because I was afraid that I would fail at being responsible. I was impulsive because I didn't know what I wanted, and I was desperate to fill the ever-expanding void that gnawed away at my insides.

The bottom line is, I believed that these self-damaging behaviours were as impulsive as they were out of my control. They were what I did to cope, to survive, to live, to exist and to die. It was how it was: the perpetuation of a default self-defeating, self-destructive, helpless state of being.

CAUGHT OFF-GUARD

In the shadows
there lurk
terrific horrors;
beasts hard at work.

For a brief moment
still, silent,
      possibly not there...
then, the feeling
   of a slither
and that sense
   of despair.

And the slow, tight darkness
becomes your only witness

to the terror
and the havoc
that has caught you
 unawares
  again.

ACCIDENTS DO HAPPEN

Silly me – I tripped again,
and I'd only just got up
from my last fall,
just minutes before,
and soon I'll trip again.
Stupid – as I saw it coming
and, stupid, stood and stared.
I waited for the blow to strike
and I almost didn't care.
Clumsy me – I fell
and pulled down
everything around me.
And now I sit quite gormless
while my eyes shift
through the debris.
Silly, still, I get back up
and wonder why I bother,
as I've barely caught my balance
from my last fall
and I realise too late
I'm going down with yet another.

HUNGRY, AND HUNGRY STILL

For one such as I
there is no such thing
as enough.
Nothing is enough,
Everything is not enough.
For I am hungry
and hungry still
for more and more
of what may, what will,
satisfy my appetite
for more, and even more.
But even more
is not enough
for one such as I;
for I am hungry
and hungry still.

DO NOT DISTURB

I'm busy screwing up my life
Please don't interrupt me.
I need a bit of peace and quiet
To do it properly.

I can't stand people hanging round
Trying to tell me not to,
Trying to convert my head
To think the way that they do.

I deal with things my own way
Please let me carry on.
I'll be with you in just a while
When everybody's gone.

I need a little privacy
Please look the other way;
Pretend you didn't see me
Screwing up another day.

As it turns out, I was not as helpless as I believed for
25 years; I just didn't know *how* to help myself, or why
I should even bother. The more I understood about
myself, and why I felt the way I did about life and my
place in it, the more I was able to comprehend that
change *was* possible.

Another bane of my time spent in the Therapeutic
Community was the proverbial 'toolbox' that we would
apparently be leaving with. The facilitators told us we
were being equipped with self-regulatory and social
skills that would be readily at hand – inside our toolbox.
You would think they were paid commission to sell
these things to us and I, for one, was characteristically
suspicious of their smooth sales talk.

Seriously, did they not realise just how hard it
actually was not to be impulsive? As it happens, I think
they did!

All the seemingly futile distractions that we were
encouraged to find as alternatives to self-damaging
behaviours have proved themselves invaluable in

managing my impulses: write in my notebook; phone a friend; watch a film; take a walk; read a magazine; have a cup of tea – anything to stave off the urges to self-destruct, and allow myself to pause.

At the time, all of these suggestions felt as though I was being offered a water pistol to defend myself against guerrilla warfare and yet, somehow, they work. Nobody promised that change would happen overnight, which is why, I suppose, we were sent home after 18 months with a wealth of strategies and coping mechanisms that could, with determined practice and application, transform us. I have come to discover it is not a toolbox; it is a treasure chest.

Initially, I regarded these distractions merely as a way to postpone the inevitable, and in the early days this is all they were: postponements. But I began to grasp that if I could hold off on the damaging behaviours, even for a few minutes (or seconds), and if I could postpone it a bit longer the next time, I might – eventually – be able to suspend them indefinitely.

It is incredibly uncomfortable, even now, to sit tight and not be reactive when all hell is breaking loose inside. When panic, anger, fear or pain threaten to destroy you from the inside out with not a second's notice, it is frighteningly easy to reach for a lifelong trustworthy strategy (such as self-mutilation) that reverses the process and destroys you from the outside in; the relief is palpable and instant. The consequent remorse and self-hatred however is brutal and enduring, and it was worth at least one try (I reasoned) to avoid this if I could.

I am learning to tell myself that *this too shall pass,* every time I am overwhelmed by a pull towards the drastic and the devastating. Despite how strong the feelings can be, and how absolute their hold on me, I am learning that it will not last forever. If I can hold on, postpone and ultimately abandon my natural impulse just once, then I can do it again.

Whilst nobody had lied and said this would be easy, nobody said quite how hard it would be either. Although I seem to recollect somebody telling me it would be worth the effort.

Chapter 9

....

Intense and highly changeable moods, with each episode lasting from a few hours to a few days

Well is it any wonder? Given the many and complex components of borderline personality disorder, can anyone blame us for dwelling in an almost permanent state of turmoil and dysphoria?

For far too long I lived without a single shred of inner stability. I had no roots whatsoever in my own sense of self, or worth, and I spent years being tossed around in the wake of other people, and my skewed beliefs about these other people.

I flitted around like a butterfly, although I suspect even a butterfly has a purpose. I couldn't settle – I didn't want to settle. I wanted everything or I wanted nothing at all; occasionally I wanted both simultaneously. There was nothing realistic or attainable in my whimsical fancies, only arbitrary goals that were based on watching how somebody else was living their life (seemingly) successfully.

The only breaks from this tedious transitory existence came in the form of all-consuming hurricanes of rage, panic or deeper despair than was normal for me. Once the storm passed, I would return to the state of dissatisfaction and anxiety that was my home for so long.

ANYWHERE

This could be anywhere,
but it is darkness
through and through.
Suffocating black.
Premature night.
The farthest place
from truth.
This could be anywhere,
but it is always home.
Where the lies embrace me,
fond as a lover
and jealous;
The safest place
I know.

WHERE DID WE BEGIN?

Nothing is clear
any more.
Not when, nor how,
nor even what for.
How did we come
to sink so low?
When did we stop
being able to cope?
When did we wake
first, and wish we hadn't?
When did we realise
I'd rather I wasn't?

When did my normal self
turn-coat and flee?
Where did we begin
turning in to me?

A DAY IN THE LIFE...

You wake
you wish you hadn't.
You rise
but don't know why.
You wash, you dress -
why bother?
You live
you want to die.
    You eat
you wish you hadn't.
You smile
because you should.
You eat again
you can't stop now
If you could die
you would.
    You go
through all the motions.
You prove
that you're alive.
You meet all expectations
but inside
you know you've died.
    You sleep

after a fashion.
You wake
but wonder why.
You rise, you wash,
you dress, you eat...
you live
you live a lie.

RUNNING SCARED

Desperation drives me
in my haste, I know not where.
Deeper, further, weaker,
afraid of my despair.
Darkness suffocates me
as my past attends my grave
and the tender preparations
feign the closure that I crave.
Confusion overwhelms me
'til I'm frozen on the spot,
and I'm blown away by choices
while I cling to what I'm not.

My desperate attempts to be somebody I was not (and
could *never* be), no doubt contributed profoundly to
my continuous state of irritability and despair. It was
impossible to be rested when I was convinced I needed
to change and become just like Sue, Diane or even
Mark or Bill!

I would never get even the slightest whiff of stability until I dared to believe that it was okay to be me, gargantuan-sized warts and all. I would never feel settled until I learned to be comfortable in (and grateful for) my own skin.

And I could never begin to get better until I accepted that I was the only person that could make me better. And this process could never begin, until I trusted that I was worth the time and effort, deserving of compassion and capable of being 'somebody'.

The more I understand about myself, and why I am the way I am, the more I am able to accept and embrace who I am.

As I learn to stop and think, challenge my automatic thoughts, and take responsibility for myself I feel less dissatisfied and restless.

I am gradually taking back control of who I am, discovering who I want to be, and where I want to go, by allowing *me* to define *me*.

More and more I feel comfortable in my own skin, because I can see that I am not *all* wrong, or *all* bad, and that some of me is good, and right.

My perceptions of myself and others are steadily becoming less extreme as I remind myself to see more grey. Occasionally I even see the hint of a colour here and there!

It has taken years of therapy, years of searching for myself and learning to accept (if not like) what I have found, and years of daring to trust the people around me who told me I was okay, to reach this point. I can look back on my own journey and be proud of myself. I have a long way yet to go, but I have come further than I ever believed possible.

HOME

Years of pain,
And searching.
Oceans of tears,
And yearning.
Dark days,
Impossible steps,
Each leading me here;
Carrying me.
Home.

SEE THE SUN AGAIN

Another empty promise
Or, perhaps, a threat?
The sky will soon be clear
The sun shine on me yet.
The rain I loathe is safe to me
The clouds dark, but sure.
Suppose the sun shines right on me
Would life want even more?
　　Dare I close my eyes and wish;
Lift my head and trust
That I will see the sun again?
I dare not, but I must.

Epilogue

....

The official diagnosis of borderline personality disorder is not actually confirmed until we are nearing the end of our 18 months in the Therapeutic Community.

Every other Monday we had a group in which we trawled through a long and laborious questionnaire about our patterns and behaviours over the course of many years. The completed questionnaire, together with facilitators' observations of our behaviours over the course of our therapy, formed the basis of our eventual diagnosis.

In some ways it felt like quite a blow to be given this damning information as we walked out the doors. *Well done for all your hard work in therapy, however — you're screwed*, is what they might as well have said when I first realised this was the process. In hindsight though, I think I see the reasoning behind it. Not only was the diagnosis reached by a thorough evaluation, it was also presented to us once we had had the opportunity to begin to understand the disorder and taken enough tentative steps to believe that we could manage it on our own.

When I was given my diagnosis, the psychiatrist, Lisle, asked me if I would inform Complex Needs of any changes of name or address, in case they needed to contact me in the future. I remember laughing, and asking why on earth my name would change, to which Lisle replied that I might, for example get married. I laughed even harder. I honestly never believed I would ever have a relationship, let alone one stable enough that would result in marriage. I still didn't believe, even with my infinitesimal progress, that anyone would ever want to be with me, or that I would ever be well enough to be with someone.

Whilst I cannot deny that the thought of 'being with' someone appealed to me, I was not desperate for a companion. I was still mortally afraid of the damage I might do to someone susceptible enough to love me – what if I still didn't manage to control my paranoia, my anger, my suspicions, my fears and my impulses?

I was also, after all, embarking on a completely fresh relationship with my new-found self; that was good enough, and work enough for me. To be content with, rather than resigned to, the fact that I existed at all was a huge turnaround, and I was satisfied with this new status quo.

When Dawn first moved in next door to me, she was just as frightening as every other human being ever is on first impressions, as far as I was concerned.

She was confident, friendly, outgoing – everything I still believed I was not. We became friends out of a mutual need for pet-sitters on occasion, and the more I got to know her the more I felt I was falling in love. I was afraid it was the same sort of infatuation that had been inherent for most of my life; I liked her because she liked me. And yet something awakened within me whenever we spent time together.

Dawn's understanding of self-awareness, self-discovery and mental (and emotional) wellbeing was like a breath of fresh air to me, and we communicated on these deep and profound levels. I told her about my diagnosis, and she shared her own experience of being with somebody similarly 'ill', confounding my belief that I could never act on my ever-growing feelings towards her.

We talked for hours at a time, sharing wine over our fences with our respective pets on each side (highly incompatible cat and dog). The more she got to know me, the more convinced she was that I would be able to hold down a relationship: that someone would want me, and I *was* capable of being with that someone. She was determined and adamant that I could do it. I was equally determined and adamant that I could not.

Little did Dawn know that her encouragements would eventually lead back to her. I was utterly smitten, but not in the usual borderline way. My love felt, for the first time ever, healthy, genuine and like I had always imagined this sort of love should feel.

We are now married (very happily I hasten to add), and our love and understanding grows deeper every day.

For almost 40 years I didn't once, in my wildest imaginings, believe that I would ever say this, but I am in a balanced, healthy and mutually respectful and trusting relationship.

This change in circumstances is important, not just because the psychiatrist will know where to find me should the need arise, but because here is tangible, irrefutable proof that the work I have done has borne fruit, and that the road to recovery is worth the slog; there was always hope, I just had to dare to believe it.

I am not perfect, and that is okay. I am still working on myself, and probably always will be, but I am managing myself and taking responsibility for myself, and that is amazing.

I believe I can keep getting better, and I know I am worth the effort, and that is an incredibly frightening and remarkably brave statement for me to make.

I am loved by the people who have walked this (often treacherous and most certainly painful and tedious) journey with me. And I am (most of the time) loved by myself, and that is nothing short of a miracle.

ONE STEP AT A TIME

One step, then take a break –
a few days, to recover.
One step, then rest
before embarking on another.

One step, then catch your breath
regather your composure.
One step – you can't give up –
grit your teeth and take one more.

One step, that's all you need
to make it to the next one.
One step, and soon you'll see
how far you've nearly come.

Tracy Barker is no stranger to therapy – counselling, psychotherapy, psychiatric assessments, even research-based therapy, short-term and long-term. But it was the 18 months spent in a full-time therapeutic community that had the most lasting and life-changing influence. She spent the next few years building on her new foundations, becoming an expert by experience on how to live with and manage borderline personality disorder. Now Tracy is happily married and enjoys writing, blending in with society and exploring the countryside with her two dogs somewhere near Oxford. This is her first book.